CHAPTER ONE
WINNERS ENDURE IT ALL AND
STILL DO MORE!

The world favors those who persevere and act in bold ways while taking calculated risks. And winners somehow innately know and live this universal law of success and good luck. Winners consistently find ways to show bravery by enduring fear, pain, discomfort, and uncertainty. And on top of managing all of that, they still somehow manage to do even more…

I can remember a time when I once overheard some sage advice from a mother to her daughter. Sadly, the daughter's world was falling apart right in front of her own eyes, and she couldn't seem to do a thing to stop it. You know that old saying that when it rains, it pours? Well, it was pouring heavily and sadly soaking this teenage girl. I could see that this unfortunate stroke of bad luck was tearing this girl and her mother apart.

But somehow amid this ferocious storm, the girl's mother gently told her daughter that all she had to do was just to make one small move in the right direction, and eventually, everything will somehow work itself out. That's it! Only one little step in the right direction. Instead of just sitting there paralyzed by fear and pain, one small move in the right direction is almost always the answer to our most daunting problems.

I always like to say that motion creates emotion! Do one tiny thing. Take one small step! Move your body in some way toward something better than the present. Do this, and you'll find the emotional energy to continue to do this and even more. Keep doing this, and someday when you finally pause to smell the roses, you'll marvel at how far you've traveled. You'll be absolutely amazed and lost in wonderment at the exciting journey that you almost didn't take just because things seemed too hard back then when you were weaker.

Furthermore, you'll be incredibly proud when you look in the mirror and see the type of person you have become. You'll finally feel lucky and forget about whatever problems you used to have. Also, you'll be confident in knowing that from now on, you'll be able to handle whatever curve balls life throws at you.

It won't be easy, though! It never is easy, because our Creator is more concerned about our character than our comfort. Remember, the biggest and best trees have endured the strongest winds. And the hottest fires have shaped the strongest and best steel. Don't fight it. Go with it. Let life's trials and tribulations mold you into that best woman or man of steel possible. Let life turn you into that marvelous superhero that you were meant to be.

Now frustration beaters, as my Granddaddy always said, "Go learn, lead, and lay the way to a better world for all of us. Remember what Franklin Delano Roosevelt said back during one of this country's most trying periods in our modern history. "You have nothing to fear, but fear itself." And, "Above all else, do something!" Follow FDR's advice, and you too will become one of those winners that dare to endure fear, pain, discomfort, and uncertainty, and still do more. And once again, thanks in advance for all that you do, and all that you will do…

CHAPTER TWO
WINNING IS LIKE SCIENCE!

Have you ever heard of a thing called potential energy? How about kinetic energy? What about the laws of science that say an object at rest tends to stay at rest, and an object in motion manages to stay in motion? Of course, you have! Anybody who has ever attended school has at least heard of these rules of science.

So right about now, you're probably wondering what all these fancy science terms and laws dealing with motion and friction and science stuff have to do with leadership and winning, aren't you? Well, the simple answer is EVERYTHING!

Let me explain what I'm talking about. Let's look at an example of trying to push a stalled car. Some of us already know that the hardest part of putting a stalled car at rest into motion is to get it out of a dead stop. Once we budge that car just a little bit and the tires start to roll slowly, then even a 2,000-pound automobile becomes easy to continue to push and move as long as we don't encounter any hills, right? The hardest part of moving the stalled car is the beginning. The rest of the motion becomes easy due to momentum or kinetic energy.

Well, I'm here today to tell you about your potential energy and that establishing behaviors and habits of leadership and winning are also difficult in the beginning. But, once we initiate a pattern of productive behaviors, we'll gain some momentum, and then leadership and victory will come to us much more frequently and much easier than it did before pursuing this movement toward leadership and winning. You see, leadership and winning are just like pushing that car. It's hard in the beginning, and then much more manageable after we get some movement.

So the biggest obstacle is really just getting started. And now that we know this scientific winning principal, we can no longer let the START stop us. We can no longer just allow life to happen to us. And we can no longer just blindly turn over control of our future, our dreams, and our destiny to our own weak and flawed human natural tendencies of laziness and indifference when dealing with difficult things.

Throughout human existence, we humans have developed complex, intellectual brains. And even though we're still in a sense primordial emotional creatures, we're also modern-day humans that now can think our way out of some bad habits. Intellectually, we should be able to see through the smoke screens and false reasons our flawed human nature throws at us in the feelings of laziness and indifference.

You see, here's the problem. Our own human nature wants to keep us in inertia. That's another fancy science term that in a sense, means not moving forward towards our goals and dreams. Our brains do this to us because it thinks it's saving life energy just in case a famine comes someday soon... I don't think a famine is happening, what do you think?

In addition, because we are also thinking creatures, we should be able to intellectualize, especially after reading this article, that the beginning or the START is the hardest part of success and winning. But thankfully, it's not an impossible part of succeeding and winning.

And once we do the tiniest, littlest thing to create movement in the right direction, momentum kicks in and then the next small step is that much easier. String together a bunch of these puny successful steps, and we'll fire up our primordial emotions and instincts to assist our modern-day intellect.

This dynamic duel of past and present will then want to step on the gas and shift our human thinking, emotional bodies into overdrive in an attempt to quickly succeed and feel self-satisfaction. This behavior falls in line with the old pain-pleasure principle. Once we reach this pleasurable golden place in our minds and hearts, then not even the hills will be able to stop us!

Now frustration beaters, as my Granddaddy always said, "Go learn, lead, and lay the way to a better world for all of us." Remember that winning is like a science. It takes more effort to put it into motion than to keep it going. And once again, thanks in advance for all that you do, and all that you will do...

CHAPTER THREE
WINNING TAKES AWAY THE PAIN!

A few years ago, after reading a pretty interesting book on the history and success of McDonald's, I decided to visit a local McDonald's to do some real live in-person research. I found what looked like the owner by the soda machine as I was filling up my cup. This was my chance, I thought. After he confirmed that he was indeed the owner, I asked this older gentleman what it was like back during the early days of his McDonald's ownership and management.

He shared with me that if someone had told him up front what owning and operating a McDonald's restaurant was really going to be like, then he most likely would have turned and run away and never looked back.

I was a little shocked by this shaky answer from such a successful man, so I pried a little more. "What do you mean?" I asked. "Was it really that bad?"

He smiled and told me that it was way more difficult and way more painful than anything that he had ever done before.

"Well, how about now?" I asked.

He smiled again and pointed toward the parking lot. My eyes were drawn to the center of the parking lot where a mint-condition, shiny, red convertible Chevy Corvette sat. It was a beautiful automobile, and there was no way one's eyes couldn't have been drawn to it. Sweet, I thought to myself.

Well, I guess I had my answer, I surmised. If his early days as a McDonald's owner and the operator had been painful and difficult, it sure didn't appear that way now. This older gentleman was smiling and actually looked like he was having fun. He seemed like he didn't have a care in the world as he just stood there radiating joy and happiness. Life and his career were obviously good!

I thanked him for his time and the profound life lesson I had just learned as I shook his hand and said good-bye so I could eat my meal and drink my Coke with a smile on my face. The old man started out in the direction of his office in the back of the store, and then stopped and waved good-bye as he hollered out to stop by again sometime.

When I finally drove my not-quite-so mint-condition and not-so-shiny red Chevy Cavalier home that day, I couldn't help but wonder about this old man and the life-lesson he had just shared with me. He seemed so happy with what he was doing now, and the owner was very friendly as he so graciously took time out of his day to spend it talking to me.

As I continued to sip on what was left of my Coca Cola and mull over this man's present success and happiness stemming from a difficult start, I couldn't help but wonder if his lessons could also apply to people who weren't as old and as experienced. Could much younger and inexperienced people like my friends and I also benefit from surviving a rocky start? I think so.

So while gripping my steering wheel with one hand and using the other to sip my soda, my mind wandered again as it often does to other important things in my life. A big part of my life at the time was the sport of wrestling. I had been a high school wrestling star and was presently coaching a local high school wrestling team.

While driving home from my pleasant experience at McDonald's with the elderly owner, I wondered if someone had told me right up front everything that it would take to succeed in the sport of wrestling, would have turned and run away without looking back like that McDonald's owner had told me earlier that he would have.

My answer, just like his, was YES. I wondered if the early years of wrestling were way more difficult and way more painful than anything else I had done before. And again my answer was, YES!

Next, my mind wandered to the relaxed, carefree older gentleman's smile and the fun he seemed to be having in the present while simultaneously reaping large rewards for his past efforts. I tried to tie that to my life and wondered if my journey as a young wrestling coach was somehow like his as an owner and operator of McDonald's. And once again, my answer was, YES!

Over the years, wrestling had become easy for me. It was even fun now. It didn't seem like work at all. And it was also gratifying for me too as I watched my young wrestlers develop into young men who made their families and schools proud of them.

So it's true then, anybody can be a winner at any age, and winning actually does take away the pain. In addition, winning also usually leaves a smile in its wake as the past pain and difficulty of learning is washed aside by victory, and the great feeling of self-satisfaction in a job well done!

Now frustration beaters, as my Granddaddy always said, "Go learn, lead, and lay the way to a better world for all of us." Remember, nothing worthwhile will be easy or handed to you. We all have to work for it and deal with uncertainty. And sometimes that's painful. But don't sweat it because winning takes away a lot of the pain. And once again, thanks in advance for all that you do, and all that you will do...

CHAPTER FOUR
YOU KNOW WHAT TO DO!

I once heard a health and fitness guru tell his audience the secret to weight-loss. He said it was to burn more calories than they consume. That's it! It's that simple! Burn more calories than you consume! That was it! That was the simple and profound advice from the sage on the stage that these people paid good money to come to listen to and learn from.

But yet, even with their own money invested in hearing this expert, most still won't follow his sought after advice. The funny thing is that after failing to follow through on the recommendation of the guru, many of these same people then wonder why they can't lose that last stubborn ten pounds! Amazing, isn't it? Sometimes we're our own worst enemies, aren't we?

Well, guess what? A lot of us are living a life like this scenario mentioned above. Although our weaknesses may be in a different area than weight-loss, I am pretty sure that every one of us has a flaw somewhere. And sadly, are suffering a little bit from their inability to follow through on others' simple, but profound advice.

At this moment I can't help but think of how many times one of my students or even my own children have said, "I know. I know. You don't have to tell me again because I already know." At that point, I usually find myself replying back with something equally trite and useless like, "Well then, why aren't you doing it?" Sound familiar? Yeah, I thought so…

If we really stop and think about it, with today's easy fingertip access to information through the Internet, social media, as well as all the opportunities we have for human contact, most of us probably already do know what to do to become successful and win in the game of life. And if we don't know what to do to win, then I'm sure we can easily find the information we need, right?

So then, why aren't more of us already successful winners? Why is there such a big knowing and doing gap? Why is the difference so big and obvious that a couple of college professors have already written a book on this exact topic of the knowing and doing gap?

Well, a lot of our problems come down to just normal human nature of laziness and indifference. We have to fight our human nature and not let our common enemy of *good enough* stop us from the greatness of losing that last ten pounds, or whatever else it is that we desire to do.

Another tool we could use to get beyond our human nature of laziness, indifference, and *good enough* is the old psychological pain and pleasure principle. We have to stop letting the thought of pain and pleasure use and abuse us. We need to stand up to this powerful dual, lasso them, and then make this incredible human psychological force of pain and pleasure work for us rather than against us so that we can take charge and shape the future that we want.

We have to stop being afraid of soaring high above into the stratosphere of success and winning. We have to stop worrying about the pain that might be involved in taking a new path. Instead, we have to turn our human nature around and learn to associate painfulness to a life of mediocrity and *good enough* where people are always telling us what to do, and then, in self-defense, we often find ourselves firing back, "I know. I know. You don't have to keep telling me because I already know what to do."

This all-too-common scenario of, "I know. I know," should become too painful for us to endure any more. None of us should ever want to fall helplessly into that crevice of the knowing and doing gap again. All of us should want to operate on a higher plane where we not only know what to do, but we also take charge of our lives, and we become the bosses of our future and creators of our own destiny by doing what we know!

Now frustration beaters, as my Granddaddy always said, "Go learn, lead, and lay the way to a better world for all of us." Beware of knowing what to do, but not doing it. Living in this gap is what everybody else does, but not you. Not anymore. And once again, thanks in advance for all that you do, and all that you will do…

CHAPTER FIVE
NOTHING CAN REPLACE DOING
THE WORK!

Nothing can replace doing the work. You see, it's in doing the work that we eventually become so familiar with what we're doing that we no longer have to focus 100% of our energy anymore to just completing the sequential steps of a particular task. At this point in our progress and proficiency, we now have some energy left over to look at our task in new ways. And looking at things in new ways helps us find some remarkable success, which creates the perfect scenario for our creative genius to finally come to the surface.

Beware though, chances are that our creative genius will most likely stay put if we stay put. Our talent is usually buried just beneath the surface until we have done enough work to create the perfect environment for our new creative life to hatch.

Think of it this way, all our hard work and all of those long hours can be seen as an incubator for our future amazing selves. If we continually feed our inner seeds of greatness, our work ethic, and carefully create and caress the perfect birthing conditions for our creative genius to hatch, then our efforts will be richly rewarded. I guarantee that!

In contrast, though, if we don't do the work, and don't create the perfect environment to foster our creative genius... well... then I guess we will never know what could have been... Ah... So sad... Don't you agree?

Now I've told you in previous writings that it takes about 10,000 hours of doing a particular task to get really good at it so that you can compete on the national level. And I have also told you that if you want to compete on the international level, then we're going to need about 15,000 hours of practice.

For example, Malcolm Gladwell talks about the reason the Beatles made it big in his book, *Outliers*. Put simply, the Beatles played more music than any other band. The Beatles performed live in Hamburg, Germany more than 1,200 times from 1960-1964, usually playing seven hours a night while most other music groups only played about two or three hours a night.

Thus, the Beatles were able to amass more than 10,000 hours of practice much quicker than their competitors. When they finally returned to England, they rocked the house and then took their show on the road to the United States where they eventually changed the U.S. music industry forever.

Furthermore, Malcolm Gladwell's book *Outliers* also talks about Bill Gates. Gladwell talks about all the hours Bill Gates spent in middle school and then high school tinkering with computers during a time when most people barely had any access at all to computers. Now, I think we all know how Bill Gates' hard work and long hours around computers turned out. It turned out to be a $50 billion empire, didn't it?

As a matter of fact, I challenge anyone of you to show me one person that made it big on their own who didn't put in the long hours and a whole lot of hard work; most likely, 10,000 hours of hard work. Come to think of it, I can save you a whole lot of time and a whole lot of energy right now by just telling you that that person doesn't exist. Bottom line: Nothing can replace doing the work.

Now frustration beaters, as my Granddaddy always said, "Go learn, lead, and lay the way to a better world for all of us." Remember, nothing can replace doing the work. So go ahead and do the work, and then get ready to reap the creative rewards of the labors of your love. And once again, thanks in advance for all that you do, and all that you will do…

CHAPTER SIX
YOU CAN HAVE ANYTHING
YOU WANT!

You can have anything you want, if you want it bad enough, and are willing to pay the price. That's excellent news, isn't it? So the world is our oyster after all, right? Wow! This is awesome! I'm so excited. I can't believe that we can literally have anything that our little hearts desire! So let's go get what we want and wish for!

Wait. Hold on a minute. This sounds too good to be true, doesn't it? If we can have anything that we want, then why don't more of us already have more of the things that we want? And why aren't more of us humans happier if we could genuinely have anything we want?

Well, after some pondering, I think the real issue here isn't the validity of having anything we want. I think our real challenge, and the thing that keeps a lot of us from being as happy as we want to be is that most of us haven't figured out what we truly want in life, and what we truly want out of life, yet.

You see, we are programmed continuously to think and live our lives in a certain way by others from the moment we are born until the moment we die. Think about this for a moment. We're brought into this world and if we aren't crying as loud as the doctor thinks we should be then someone slaps our little behinds to make us cry out louder. Did we really want to cry out even louder at that exact moment? Apparently not or we would have already been doing it on our own!

From that spanking introduction into this new world, we're always told what to do and want we "should want" in our lives. Our parents tell us what to do and what we should want. Our siblings tell us what to do and what to want. Our teachers and coaches tell us what to do and what to want. Even our friends tell us what to do and what to want.

And then eventually, our spouses and then the needs of our own children tell us what to do and what to want.

Oh, yeah, let's not forget about Hollywood and Wall Street. They are always telling us what to do and what to want too by bombarding us with their advertising and easy financing. They are continually showing us how easy life would be if we just bought their newest product, and looked and behaved more like them. Hint: watch out for their subliminal messages; they're very powerful human programmers. I know this because I did a college presentation on this once.

In retrospect, sadly, most of us haven't really been given a chance yet to discover who we indeed are. Also, most of us have been led to believe that life should be easy. Just do what you're told and we won't have any problems, right? Sound familiar? It sure does! Well, sorry guys, but we've all have been programmed to think and want and behave like others have wanted us to for most of our lives.

The first thing we're going to do to reprogram ourselves more to our own liking rather than others' liking so we can find out who we truly are, and what we truly want in life. One way to do this is to spend some more time alone in a quiet place thinking about our lives. We'll also need to try some new things and have some new experiences, like meeting some new people who will help us to think anew and have a fresh perspective on life. Hopefully, after doing some of these things I just mentioned, we will be able to gain some valuable insight on who we are and what kind of person we want to become, as well as what we want in life and out of life.

After we have figured out for ourselves what kind of person we want to become, then we should WANT to do almost anything, and take nearly any amount of time to get there and BE that kind of person! Unfortunately, it won't be quick though, nor will it be easy like Hollywood and Wall Street has promised us.

Now if we're not willing to go through that kind of challenging and exhilarating journey, then we probably need to do some more work in figuring out what we truly want. You see, surprisingly the magical formula or this new programming is being offered to us free of charge, so we need to grab it and hold on to it tightly. Trust me, you're going to like the new you. So here is the simple, but the not easy formula to reprogram ourselves: know what we want and then work for it no matter how long it takes or how hard it is, and it, whatever it is, will eventually become ours.

Now frustration beaters, as my Granddaddy always said, "Go learn, lead, and lay the way to a better world for all of us." Remember, we can have anything we want if we want it bad enough, and are willing to pay the price. Here's a little caveat though; let's not sweat it if we don't quite hit our goals because the person we become through our own individual journeys is really the real prize. And now once again, thanks in advance for all that you do, and all that you will do...

CHAPTER SEVEN
YOU ARE ALREADY HALFWAY THERE!

Everybody is good at something. Everybody has at least one thing that they like to spend their energy and time on. This one thing is not the same things for all of us. But, regardless of our individual human differences, we all still have that one unique thing that we love to do and are good at. Are you getting what I'm saying here? I hope I'm showing you that you are good at something. I want to help you understand that IQ and intelligence are not static or narrow in scope like some past generations had once thought. And that's good news for all of us because every one of us is smart and can succeed in some way!

IQ, intelligence, and success mean many different things for many different people. We all have a powerful IQ, and we all have a vast amount of intelligence in our own unique ways because every one of us is unique, special, experienced, and successful in our own individual ways.

Now I'm sure you've already heard the saying that God doesn't make junk. Well, we know God made you so you can't be junk regardless of whatever you're going through at the moment or what some insecure people may be telling you. So buck up, little camper; our Creator has special plans for you.

I know for a fact that if you look hard and long enough at yourself, you'll see that you are good at something. And it's usually something that you spend a lot of your free time on and enjoy doing.

Now let me ask you this next question. If our Creator gave you enough passion, enthusiasm, skills, and intelligence to be good with at least one thing, then don't you think that our Creator would want you to take those passions and talents and to use them to broaden your horizon by applying them to a second thing? How about a third, or even fourth thing? Maybe our Creator wants you to apply your specialty to all areas of your life… Hmm… Imagine that!

Hey, our Creator doesn't think small and neither should you! You're already good at something. So now use what you know and go be good at something else too! Trust me; this is a step forward that will take your life in the right direction. Applying yourself and the skills you have already gained doing your "one thing" more thoroughly will help you to become much happier eventually, fulfilled, and successful in the long run.

Now you just have to find the courage to take this chance on yourself. Just do it! Trust yourself. Invest in yourself. And broaden your horizon and your life experiences. Believe me, it will be worth it!

Now frustration beaters, as my Granddaddy always said, "Go learn, lead, and lay the way to a better world for all of us." Don't let tough times get you down and steal your faith in yourself. Always remember that you are already halfway there. Just take the skills and ambitions that you have already learned in one area of your life and transfer them over to another, and then eventually, all areas of your life! And once again, thanks in advance for all that you do, and all that you will do...

CHAPTER EIGHT
ABOVE ALL DO SOMETHING

FDR or Franklin Delano Roosevelt was trapped in a wheelchair and couldn't walk or even stand on his own without assistance from others. This was also during a time when people looked down on others with handicaps. But, astonishingly, somehow FDR managed to get elected four times as President of the United States of America and become one of the most powerful men in the world!

How did FDR who couldn't even stand, rise to those heights?

Well, for one thing, he didn't let polio keep him flat on his back doing "nothing." Instead, he overcame the limitations of his physical disability because he consciously decided to do "something" about it!

Wheelchair-bound FDR became our 32nd President of the United States in 1933 during the worst financial crisis this country has ever seen. In addition to those economic problems, the country was also in social and political upheaval. People were starving to death, many families couldn't afford to stay together, and people were screaming that our social, political, and economic system of capitalism wasn't working anymore.

Some people wanted our long-standing capitalistic system to be overthrown and replaced with something more concerned with people rather than just making another buck and creating another Rockefeller-like robber baron.

Socialism and even communism were real threats to our country at this time in history while so many people were out of work, hungry, and desperate. These tough times were the perfect breeding ground for a dictator to come to life who could succeed in replacing the slower moving and less efficient democratic system of government with a much more effective totalitarian regime of government like Germany had with Adolf Hitler, and Russia had with Joseph Stalin.

This was a big... no, let's say HUGE mess that FDR rolled his wheelchair into by becoming President of the United States during the Great Depression and coming world war.

What could one man, who was trying his best to hide his disability from the American people for fear of what they may think, do against a whole system that seemed like it was about to collapse and the rising dictators on the horizon? What could he do about the political extremes at both ends of the political spectrum of this country that were always at each other's throats and wanted the country to move only toward their vision of what it should be?

Well, FDR did "something," and then he did a lot more "somethings" during his presidency. And those "somethings" might have just saved this country from revolution, as well as protect our capitalistic and democratic systems in the 1930s. FDR deftly injected a few very controversial socialistic social programs into our American way of life without entirely changing our capitalistic system. One of these social programs is the social security program that is still around today and still benefits millions.

Also, FDR gave the ordinary person some hope that they were going to make it through The Great Depression because now the common person found a little bit money in their pockets and a little bit of food in their bellies thanks to his programs.

Next, things got even more complicated for FDR. Entering into the 1940s, while still in the tail end of the Great Depression, Adolf Hitler was waging war over in Europe and causing all sorts of trouble on our Eastern Front with his submarines in the Atlantic Ocean. Simultaneously, an equally dangerous foe attacked us on our Western Front when Japan bombed Pearl Harbor on December 7, 1941.

Once again facing the overwhelming odds, and knowing that our country was filled with peace-loving pacifists who didn't want to fight way over there. Furthermore, we were still financially struggling, and our military wasn't adequately equipped or trained for a two-front war. What could one man who was held a prisoner in a wheelchair possibly do about adversaries as dangerous and effective as Hitler and Japan?

Well, once again, FDR did "something," and then he did a lot more "somethings" that helped convert this country into the arsenal of democracy it became. Our country's factories pulled off the Production Miracle. Our factories were able to fully equip our military and then replace anything of ours that either Hitler of Japan destroyed.

Fortunately for us, Germany and Japan's factories weren't able to do the same during WWII. We Americans fought bravely overseas while our factories out-produced Germany and Japan on the home front with a never-ending source of supplies, commitment, and bravery of their own.

Now, I doubt that anyone of us is facing the kind of problems that FDR faced way back in the 1930s and 1940s. However, I can bet every one of us is facing some kind of issues in our lives. And I can probably assume that most of us aren't able to clearly see all the right answers to all of our problems. Well, I'm here to tell you not to sweat the small stuff, and it's all small stuff now, right? So relax, and I'll explain.

Are you ready? Good. Let's do this then. For anything that you're struggling with and contemplating on what to do next, here is your answer: do "something" and once you have done "something," then you have gotten that much closer to the right solution to your problems. Now continue and keep doing a bunch of "somethings". If you do this, I'm sure you'll inch your way closer and closer to the right answers. And things will eventually work themselves out. Trust me! You'll see!

Now frustration beaters, as my Granddaddy always said, "Go learn, lead, and lay the way to a better world for all of us." Remember, what FDR said during our two worst crises in modern U.S. history. "Above all, do something!" So go ahead. Get out there and do "something." And make that "something" something positive and productive that will help make this place a better place for us all to live. And once again, thanks in advance for all that you do, and all that you will do...

CHAPTER NINE
YOU MUST DO THE THINGS THAT YOU
DO NOT THINK YOU CAN DO!

S ome people say First Lady Eleanor Roosevelt ran the White House and this country on the days that President Franklin Delano Roosevelt wasn't feeling up to it due to his illness with polio. If she did run this country, then I'd say that we'd all have to agree that Eleanor Roosevelt was a pretty amazing woman, as well as a very powerful one too! It would also have appeared that she was in a position that would have been very foreign and maybe even nearly impossible for any woman to do during that time in our country's history when women were still looked down on as inferior to men, and not suitable for politics.

Also, I'm reasonably sure that most women of the 1930s and 1940s probably thought that neither they nor any other woman of their times could do the things that Eleanor Roosevelt did. But guess what? She did those undoable things. And she did them without asking for anyone's permission to do them. She saw a need, and she fulfilled that need. And believe it or not, many others since Eleanor have followed her lead and done what many thought may have seemed impossible, or at least, not allowed. But, regardless, these amazing people have done it anyway.

You see, the truth is that we never know what we're really capable of until we try. When we look at the problems facing us, unfortunately, our imperfect human nature tends to make mountains out of molehills, and this scares us away from attempting the task that seems impossible. Furthermore, we also tend to ask ourselves this horrible question, "Who am I to believe that I'm good enough or talented enough to do this particular thing?" This is a bad question. Don't go there.

Sadly, we tend not to give ourselves permission to try many things that we may actually end up liking, and even being good at. Even worse, if we do try some of these things, we seldom give ourselves permission to perform poorly at first and then fail if we must to learn. Any expert out there knows that you must stumble and fall a lot before you become really good at something. But, yet, we still won't do it…

Unfortunately, we also tend to give away a lot of our own power to society. Many times we will not try to do something because we think that someone will criticize us, or society will frown upon it. Come on… think back to how many times you wanted to do something, but didn't because you felt that it was something you just couldn't do without upsetting someone else.

Don't be too hard on yourself. Most of us rarely allow ourselves to feel the joy and excitement of trying something new. And if it's something that others think and say that we cannot do, well, their opinions pretty much put a nail in our coffin of adventure and experimentation to a new exciting life almost every time for most of us.

Eleanor Roosevelt didn't let the impossible stop her, and neither should we. Also, Eleanor didn't let that powerful word "NO" stop her, and neither should we. So let's go ahead and try to do that which we think we cannot do. And do it with no apologies. Let's stumble and fall if we must, but let's not sit paralyzed in that fear and failure.

Don't be complacent either. Stretch a little bit. Elongate those boundaries of human possibilities, and who knows what we may accomplish. And if we don't do this, well, then, unfortunately, we and the rest of the world may never get a chance to enjoy our gifts. But, if we forge ahead, we may change this world for the better for all!

Now, I want all of us to think of what a shame that would be if the world never got a chance to enjoy our unique gifts to it because we were afraid and felt that we weren't good enough or allowed to do it.

What a shame it would have been if Joe Dimaggio never shared his gift of baseball with the world because he thought he couldn't for some crazy reason! What a shame it would have been if Michael Jordan had never shared his gift of basketball with the world because he thought he couldn't for some crazy reason! What a shame it would have been if Venus Williams had never shared her gift of tennis with the world because she thought she couldn't for some crazy reason! What a shame it would have been if Nelson Mandela had never shared his gifts of love, forgiveness, and leadership with the world because he thought he couldn't for some crazy reason. And what a shame it would have been if Oprah Winfrey had never shared her gift with the world because she thought she couldn't for some crazy reason… I believe we are all starting to get the point by now, right?

Now frustration beaters, as my Granddaddy always said, "Go learn, lead, and lay the way to a better world for all of us." Remember what Eleanor Roosevelt said, "You must do the things that you do not think you can do." And once again, thanks in advance for all that you do, and all that you will do…

CHAPTER TEN
EVERY NOTABLE WORK IS AT
FIRST IMPOSSIBLE!

The impossible is notably, possible! This phenomenon has been proven over and over throughout history, and yet our human nature still keeps many of us from believing this is true. Thank God for a few stubborn people who refuse to give up on their dreams and convictions, and from time to time show us the real capacity of human beings. These quasi-super heroes have created real possibilities out of seemingly impossible situations! And have given the rest of us a lot of food for thought.

For example, they told Columbus over and over that the world was flat and that he would sail right off the end of the ocean if he attempted to navigate east to look for a spice trade route. People told him that what he was trying was impossible and even suicidal. Columbus wouldn't listen to them. He firmly believed in what he was about to do. And in the end, he proved that one could sail east from Europe and not fall off the end of the earth.

Now a little more than five hundred years later, we all know that Columbus ran into the Americas and not the India that he was looking for. However, thanks to Columbus, the world learned about the Americas and gained a better perspective on how big this planet really is. In addition, we all learned that the world isn't flat, and one won't sail off the end of it, too.

Now let's think about our own human accomplishments for a moment. Can we personally think of any modern-day examples of something that we may have done that might have seemed impossible just a short time ago?

For example, maybe you play sports, and just a few years ago it might have seemed impossible for you to dunk a basketball, but now you're thinking that it just might be within your reach. Maybe you might be a baseball player and only a couple of years ago it might have seemed impossible to hit a home run, but now you feel like you should swing for the fences.

Or maybe, now that you're a little bit bigger and older, does bench-pressing your body weight, or even more, seem possible to you today? Perhaps you're into theater, and singing and performing in front of a large crowd seemed terrifying to you just a few years ago, but not so today. Finally, maybe you're a senior in high school and can't believe that you're about to graduate and about to step out into that great big world... but you are...

You see, it's not just the famous people with their notable works, like Christopher Columbus, that prove daily that the impossible is possible. But notably, also every one of us that shows that the once unthinkable is possible after all. And this in itself, in our everyday lives, is very notable, too.

But, sadly, you see, the challenge for most of us is the same thing the old blind beggar explains in the famed Greek Tragedy, Oedipus Rex. The old blind beggar tells King Oedipus Rex that the king has two good eyes but still can't see that he killed his father and married his mother. While I'm sure we haven't murdered our fathers and married our mothers, I am sure that we humans are not perfect. And we tend to miss some things or not to see some things that are right in front of our faces and should be obvious to us just like they should have been apparent to King Oedipus Rex.

Now on a better note, one of the things that we fail to see and comprehend daily is our own human potential and our own human ability to do notable and seemingly impossible good things. If we choose to, we actually can do impossible things. Furthermore, we can also continue to do bigger and bigger impossible feats as we progress in life and become more and more of the type of person our Creator meant us to be.

So let's get out there and pick bigger impossibilities to conquer as Columbus did! Let's set sail and leave the safety of the harbor like Columbus did. Let's stop hugging the familiar shoreline and let's go deep as Columbus did. Let's not turn back when things get tough. And when it seems like everybody is against us and we're facing mutiny, let's do what Christopher Columbus did by not flinching and demanding, "One more day."

Now frustration beaters, as my Granddaddy always said, "Go learn, lead, and lay the way to a better world for all of us." Remember, every notable work is at first impossible. So go be notable and do the impossible. And once again, thanks in advance for all that you do, and all that you will do...

CHAPTER ELEVEN
MISTAKES SIMPLY SHOW US SOMETHING
THAT WE DIDN'T ALREADY KNOW!

Mistakes simply show us something that we didn't already know. Hmm… It sounds like those dreaded mistakes that we're so afraid of… and those dreaded mistakes that we try so hard to avoid… don't really have to be looked at as dreaded mistakes and painful experiences, after all.

Instead, we can view our mistakes through a different lens and now see a friendly, lovable mentor, or a caring, patient teacher. Or maybe even a wise and winning coach that is just trying to point something out to us that we need to know… but don't already know. We wouldn't get mad at our coaches for doing this, right?

So I guess it would be beneficial for all of us to change our paradigm of mistakes from one of a foe to one of a friend. If we're going to do this paradigm change, though, we're going to have to become mentally tougher and learn how to control our thoughts better. Remember, thoughts become things. So, if we're thinking that mistakes are really things that cause us a lot of pain, and make us feel really stupid and unlovable, then those thoughts are going to make those things come true. Minimally, our thoughts will at least help our perceptions of them feel real. And we all know that what we perceive to be true we tend to believe as a rock-solid truth… even if it isn't…

Unfortunately, once we feel these false thoughts are real, including the unlovable part, then we tend to become stressed, and end up lashing out at others because we don't feel worthy anymore of another's love. Sadly, this self-fulfilling prophesy of being unlovable will mess with our minds and get us to live up to the bad and negative that is expected of us. Eventually, we'll end up doing those things that make us unlovable.

It's a vicious cycle that feeds on itself in which we feel unlovable, so we lash out at others. And when we lash out at others, they find it tough to love us. Looking at mistakes this negative way and thus eventually feeling all this negativity is a downward spiral that we need to avoid at all costs!

The good news is that we can avoid this negativity trap by just changing or model or paradigm of what mistakes really mean to us. From now on, we have to make our thoughts toe the line in the sand in creating a new perception for ourselves about errors. We have to believe from now on that mistakes are a wise old mentor or a dear old friend from the past pointing out a few things that we don't know yet.

Furthermore, this new way of looking at mistakes will push us into taking action instead of just kicking that can of not-knowing too far down the road. Booting that can too far down the road only gives that small mound of trouble time to grow into a big mountain of misery that can eventually overshadow us and cover us in a cold funk of depressed darkness.

We can avoid the Mt. Everest shadow from over-taking us and our loved ones by just being thankful and maybe even grateful for the small mistakes that we make today. Those little mistakes of today are just pointing out some small things that we don't already know yet, and are subsequently helping us avoid the big, ugly, and nasty mistakes lurking behind tomorrow.

Now frustration beaters, as my Granddaddy always said, "Go learn, lead, and lay the way to a better world for all of us" Remember, mistakes are our friends because they just simply show us some things that we didn't already know yet. So let's control our thoughts and remember that small errors are good friends because they teach us many valuable lessons up front before real disasters can strike. And once again, thanks in advance for all that you do, and all that you will do…

CHAPTER TWELVE
GOYA- GET OFF YOUR ARSE

Nobody knows the trouble I've seen. Nobody knows my sorrow... Sorry folks, but that's just part of life. Sometimes we all feel like singing the blues with Louis Armstrong. Life doesn't always go the way we want. As a matter of fact, life rarely goes the way we want. So when we're having one of those days, and there will be a lot of them, the worst thing we can do is to become helpless, feel sorry for ourselves, and get lost in the blues.

Go ahead and observe the people around you. What's the typical reaction when things go wrong? Yup! You're right. You've seen what I've seen. When things go wrong, our peers usually get thrown off their game plan. Sadly, some of them permanently get thrown off track and can never seem to gather enough steam to get back up there and to get going again.

Another thing we've all seen our peers and family do is to complain endlessly. They'll go around telling everyone they know- and even some they don't know- about their stroke of bad luck like that's going to fix it all somehow. It doesn't fix anything. The only thing complaining does is make the monster bigger.

We can't be victims. We must be victors! We can't go telling everyone about our problems. All complaining does is give our problems more steam to work with inside of our heads. In addition, complaining also keeps us off track and off to the side, digging a rut that is dangerously getting deeper and deeper with our complaint-shovel.

When we blab our mouths to everyone we know about our troubles, the cold hard facts are that 50% of them don't really care. It's nothing personal, those people are too busy dealing with their own troubles. And the other 50% of the people may be happy to hear that we're having problems because of human jealousies.

I'm sure that everyone has heard that old saying that misery loves company, right? So those people out there that are really struggling aren't going to feel bad for us and come up with some magical solution to solve our problems. Other people that are struggling are going to be glad that we're struggling just like them. These strugglers are probably going to want to keep us around for some extra company and consoling. I think we may have something better to do than commiserating together, don't you?

Warning: if we let others, or even ourselves, keep us in our rut too long negatively complaining without taking any positive actions, inevitably the only thing we're going to accomplish is digging that rut a little bit deeper with each complaint. Sooner or later that rut is going to get deep enough to be classified as a shallow grave rather than a deep rut, and then we'll be in real trouble.

When things are going wrong, there is only one logical answer-G.O.Y.A., Get Off Your Arse! We can't sit there paralyzed like some helpless victim. We must move. We must take action. We must do something to improve our situation. Just sitting there only puts us further and further behind, and deeper and deeper in that hole. Doing something, anything, no matter how small it is, will get us moving in the right direction and eventually compound into a lot of good luck later.

Getting off our arse creates movement and motion. Motion creates mental, physical, and psychological energy to help us keep moving in the right direction. Moving in the right direction is the only way we're going to get closer to taking on our problems and bending them to our will and into new interesting, stimulating challenges. Overcoming these new challenges is how we're going to create better abilities and new opportunities for ourselves. These opportunities can open doors to a new vibrant, successful, and happy life for every one of us! Trust me. This really can happen.

Now frustration beaters, as my Granddaddy always said, "Go learn, lead, and lay the way to a better world for all of us." Remember, when things aren't going our way, let's refuse to let it get the best of us and let's promise to practice G.O.Y.A., Getting Off Your Arse to the best of our abilities. After all, Superman and Wonder Woman are called action heroes for a reason... And that's because they take action during the most challenging times. And once again, thanks in advance for all that you do, and all that you will do...

CHAPTER THIRTEEN
MOTION CREATES EMOTION!

M otion creates emotion. And emotion is the source of energy in taking on new challenges and thus succeeding in life. Have you ever played sports or even just gone for a run? How many of you have done this and have eventually found yourself getting your second wind? That's right; you know what I'm talking about. You're out there physically exerting yourself, and you're starting to feel tired, and your mind is wandering off to wondering how much longer you can take this physical exertion. You force yourself to do just a little bit more and shortly something amazing happens… you catch your second wind.

Once we catch our second wind, we feel great, and we feel like we could play or run all day long, right? What happened there? Well, we kept moving our bodies, and that eventually stirred our emotions into feeling like we were doing something worthwhile. Our emotions finally got to our mind and triggered a rationalizations mechanism where our mind went into overdrive trying to rationalize or figure out why continuing this activity is a logical thing to do.

Simply put, our minds answered back, like it always does when we present it with a question. In this case, our mind responded back that if we kept playing this sport, we could win this game and move that much closer toward the championship rounds. And maybe our brains are rationalizing that in the championship rounds are where we can earn people's respect and adoration from our success.

In regards to the running that was mentioned above, when we are feeling it, and we catch our second wind; our minds probably answered back that if we kept running, then this additional exercise would help us get in better shape. And when we are in better shape, we'll have a better chance of winning and then earning people's respect and adoration also. Or maybe we'll just feel better about ourselves, and that's a good thing, too.

Let's look at another example. Have you ever felt yourself feeling lazy? You know what I mean, that blah feeling that leaves you feeling a little blue. I bet during those blah times you just couldn't seem to muster up the energy needed to get your tired and drained body off that couch, huh? Now, what happened when a friend came by and dragged you off of the couch and out of the house to go do something? Once you finally did get off the couch, how did you find yourself feeling? That's right! Pretty good, huh? And you probably felt emotionally connected to your friend as well as the activity that you saw yourself doing once you were off that couch and up and moving.

You see, getting up and moving physically kick starts our emotions and swipes away that blah-tired blues feeling that we all get while lying all over our homemade kryptonite couch. However, once we are up off of our kryptonite couch and moving around, all of a sudden we feel more like Superman than a lifeless blob, don't we? So let's avoid that kryptonite couch so it can't suck away our superpowers anymore!

So there it is folks! It's true! Motion creates emotion. Need more proof. Just imagine our life-pumping human bloodstream. What does our blood do? That's right. It gives us life by always moving vital nutrients and oxygen to where it's needed. And if it stops for too long it could clog, and we could eventually die, right? So let's be like our life-flowing blood steam and always be moving with a purpose in life. If we don't, and we stop for too long, we also could be in jeopardy of eventually clotting up and dying out.

Hey, maybe the physical death from not moving with a purpose won't be anytime soon. But our joy and our emotional and mental life certainly won't last long in a self-induced hibernation state. We may still physically exist for a time on our kryptonite couch, but sadly we will have indeed ceased to live.

Now frustration beaters, as my Granddaddy always said, "Go learn, lead, and lay the way to a better world for all of us." Remember, motion creates emotion. And emotion is what gets us fired up to live LARGE during this precious one life that we have been so graciously given by our Creator. So let's not waste it. And once again, thanks in advance for all that you do, and all that you will do…

CHAPTER FOURTEEN
PROTECT YOUR WORD AND REPUTATION!

P lease don't ever forget that a person is only as good as their word and reputation. Be smart and always protect both your word and reputation! Think about making an excellent first impression… We only get one chance to make an excellent first impression. And our word and our reputation are going to be a big part of that first impression.

So let's fight with all that we have in us to always keep our word and preserve our good reputation. Someday we're going to need both. Hopefully, when that day comes both our word and reputation will still be fully functioning and not damaged beyond repair.

This dual task of protecting our word and reputation is really up to us. Things happen. And we all know things happen. That's just the way the world is. Unfortunately, when things do happen, many times, it becomes excruciating to keep our word. The circumstances have changed since we promised whatever it was that we promised.

Hey, remember, nothing ever stays the same, and that's precisely why we should never over-promise. Over-promising usually forces us to under-deliver when things change. Instead of over-promising, let's always under-promise so we can, more often than not, get lucky by over-delivering in good times and hopefully avoid getting so messed up in bad times.

In the end, even if everything in this crazy world that we all live in together is taken from us, we are going to find that we still have our reputation, good or bad. If we've done the right things, even during the tough times, then our word and our reputation will still be intact.

With an undamaged word and reputation, we can start over and redesign, recreate, and rebuild our life even better than we did the last time. This ability to create a new and improved masterful life can really happen, regardless of where we are starting this time. In short, we can lose everything, but yet still not lose everything because we still have our dependable word and reputation working for us. That undamaged word and reputation can help us design and create the unlimited, amazing type of life that we want to live.

In contrast, though, if the rough times do get the best of us and manage to fill our word and reputation with holes, then look out because the tough times are a long way away from being over. With a beat up and dragged down reputation, we will still have an awful lot to overcome; even when it seems like the worst should be behind us. Our word and reputation are sacred, so believe in them and care for them the way you would for something that really mattered to you. Because this does matter. And it matters a lot.

Now frustration beaters, as my Granddaddy always said, "Go learn, lead, and lay the way to a better world for all of us." Remember, a person is only as good as their word and reputation, so vigilantly guard both and fight with all you have to keep them in good working order. I know you can do this, regardless of any rough times that you may be facing. And once again, thanks in advance for all that you do, and all that you will do…

CHAPTER FIFTEEN
WE CAN'T THINK TWO THOUGHTS
AT THE SAME TIME!

Our human brain is amazing and can do just about anything that we wish it, and will it to do; except to think of two thoughts at the same exact time.

Our mind thinks of one thought after another. It does this rapid-fire kind of thinking all day long, as many of us probably already know. That little voice in our head is telling us that we can do something or that we can't do something is fed by a long train of thoughts. Our thoughts take turns as they follow one another as our train of thoughts enters the station of our minds.

All these thoughts we have every day and every minute just can't rush into our brain at the same time. Our army of thoughts is forced to play nice, by the rule of taking turns. And just like we all learned in kindergarten, taking turns is a good thing to do. In the same vein, this unwritten rule of our thoughts being forced to take turns is also a good thing to do. Whenever we notice ourselves thinking negative thoughts, and that little voice in our head is telling us that we not good enough to try something new, we have the power to end that negative thought's turn and start a new turn with a different thought.

That previous bad thought can't stay in place if we don't let it. We can fill that seat with another thought. The power to switch thoughts and give a different thought a turn is a good power to have. An even better power that we all have is that the next thought to enter our mind doesn't have to be a random thought or even the next logical thought of a like kind. The next thought can be any thought that we choose. So let's be wise and consciously choose a good empowering thought. Then let's use our superpowers to rush this "chosen" good thought up to the next spot in line with the good old V.I.P. treatment.

As long as we choose to have that good thought in our mind, then we're in the driver's seat, and that old bad thought and his bad friends can't return. As a matter of fact, no bad thoughts of any kind will be able to enter our minds because our brain just can't think of two thoughts at the same time. If the positive thoughts refuse to be evicted from the driver's seat in our minds, then the negative thoughts are just out of luck and out in the cold.

So let's train our brain to have good thoughts that fuel us and empower us with that "Can Do" Attitude! Let's have our positive thoughts hog the driver's seat of our minds so there just isn't any more room or time left over for bad thoughts. Let's take away the opportunity for bad thoughts to talk trash to us and fill our minds with lies about how we're not good enough to do something special. You see, this is a battle between good and evil that we can win! So starting right now super friends, let's train our brain to think only positive thoughts so we can win this game of life!

Now frustration beaters, as my Granddaddy always said, "Go learn, lead, and lay the way to a better world for all of us." Remember that we can't think two thoughts at the same time. Therefore, we need to train our brain to think positive thoughts, and then there won't be any room left over at that exact moment for negative thoughts. And once again, thanks in advance for all that you do, and all that you will do…

CHAPTER SIXTEEN
THOSE WHO HURT ARE HURTING!

Oh! I can't stand that person! He is so mean! Why does he always have to be such a jerk? I hope I never see him again. If he ever bothers me again, I don't know what I'll do! And it won't be my fault because he's asking for it. I'm tired of him always talking trash and saying stuff to try to hurt me.

Whoa! Hold on a second there, champ. Don't you ever forget that you are the one responsible for your own actions and reactions? Let's backtrack here for a moment. Why do you think this person is acting the way they are? Think about this for a moment while considering that all human behavior is driven by something. So, now, what do you think is driving this person's behavior?

Most likely, this person is in some kind of pain. It may be emotional pan and/or it may be physical pain. But be certain that there is some kind of pain driving this person to act out in the hurtful ways that they are towards others. Hey, it's just a fact that people who are happy with themselves and the world that they live in usually don't try to belittle others.

Now, I hear you. We all know that this is not an easy world. We all suffer from some kind of pain from time to time. And I also agree with you that this person should be bigger than their pain and not use it as an excuse to cause himself and others even more pain. I also understand that you may not want to be around this particular painful person anymore. I hear your concerns loud and clear on all of your concerns.

However, what I'm asking you here is to be bigger than all of the petty stuff and be different than the others by having some kind of understanding and empathy for the person in pain. Believe it or not, you may be some hurting and hurtful person's only chance today at turning things around.

You see most others probably won't recognize that this hurtful person is hurting, but now you do. Most people will probably think that this person is just a jerk, but now you know different. I'm not saying you have to make this individual your own personal project, and spend all your time and energy on him. You don't have to be his verbal or physical punching bag. Nor do you have to be a martyr. Being a martyr is over-rated anyway.

But, what I'm asking is that you don't go out of your way to avoid this hurting and hurtful person. And when your paths cross, don't add to that path of destruction with more scornful and scorching words. Instead, just pause, smile, and try to better understand this hurting and hurtful person. And if you can muster up the courage and wisdom to do so, then please say a few kind words. Or maybe even do something nice for the pain-in-the-butt person. This may be the only act of kindness that this person receives today.

Your act of kindness may be the only gentle and good thing that this hurting and hurtful person has received in a long time. And this little sliver of humanity may be the spark that he holds onto during his darkest hours. This tiny sliver of humanity may someday ignite a new, kinder, and more productive lifestyle for this person. Think of the possibilities your small act of kindness can bring to this person and how it can lessen his potential path of destruction. If your small act of kindness doesn't work, then you haven't really lost anything, have you? But… what if it does work?

Now frustration beaters, as my Granddaddy always said, "Go learn, lead, and lay the way to a better world for all of us." Remember that people who hurt are hurting. You have the opportunity to help him break free of this destructive behavior if you dare to understand and help him out. Oh, by the way, have I ever told you that empathy is one of the strongest intelligences? Hmm… And once again, thanks in advance for all that you do, and all that you will do…

CHAPTER SEVENTEEN
I SHALL ALLOW NO MAN TO BELITTLE MY SOUL BY MAKING ME HATE HIM!

We must be extra careful not to give away our powers, especially to undeserving people! Yes. We have powers; extraordinary powers, and lots of them, too. And yes we do have the ability to hold on to these special powers even when dealing with people who are trying to make us feel small.

Some people have a way of making us angry, scared, and crazy. Sometimes we feel like we can't take another minute of that particular person. However, we must never allow this person to belittle our souls by making us hate him or her. We cannot allow ourselves to be victimized by this person or anyone else. We must remember that going forward we are a victor, not a victim.

Here's the deal... We live in an imperfect world where sometimes people are going to do things we don't like that may even cause us some harm. Some people will accidentally hurt us, while others will intentionally hurt us. Yes... Some people will try to hurt us on purpose. Let's not get too mad about this injustice, though. Let's not hate the hurter. They are just trying to make erroneous attempts to regain some of their own powers in attempting to steal some of our powers.

What the big meanies, who are trying to ruffle our feathers, don't understand is that personal power can be elusive. Trying to steal others' powers is always an inferior method for creating one's own.

Sadly, some people just don't know how to create their own feelings of power and control. In addition, some of these same people feel weak, insecure, and out of control. They mistakenly believe that making us mad gives them back a sense of control and power, however false it may be.

It's sad, isn't it? So let's not help them continue down this wrong road of harassing and bullying others. Let's stand on the higher ground of love, and help these people who don't know how to help themselves. Ironically, by helping them and refusing to hate them, we'll be helping ourselves too, believe it or not.

Now to help us all get a better grasp on how silly it is to give away our powers, especially to the non-deserving, let's all participate in this trivial little exercise. Let's imagine some small child is playing with his or her small action figure toys. These action figure toys could be Superman, Spiderman, Wonder Woman, Batman, G.I. Joe, or whoever else we can think of, okay?

Imagine a small child picking up the action figures and making them hit each other and crash into each other until they fall powerlessly to the ground. Can you picture this? Good. It's kind of silly, and it's something we've all seen before, right?

Now, remember that person whom we'd love to hate, and would hate to love? Good. Well, that person who drives us crazy and sometimes even makes us feel small is really the tiny child that we just envisioned. Now, I've already told you that we all have powers, so that makes us at least some kind of big superheroes in the real world, right?

However, don't you agree that we're much bigger than those small action figures that don't have any real world powers? And don't you also think that we, as big superheroes, are way too good to let that small child disguised as that adult person who drives us crazy shrink us down to the size of those small lifeless action figures that he or she just manipulated and smashed around? Why would any of us allow that person to get the best of us by crashing us into things and then having us powerlessly fall to the ground like some old used up toys? We wouldn't, right?

Dang right! We're too good for that child's play! We're real-life superheroes, with real-life unlimited superpowers. And we won't let some big immature kid get the best of us anymore! We'll refuse to give away our powers and the essence of whom we really are to a person that is just trying to irk us.

We won't hate this person, regardless of how big, or mean, irritating, or underserving this person may be. No matter how much they seem to deserve it, we'll be smarter and just rise above it all. And regarding those people that mistakenly or unknowingly hurt us... Oh well. We'll look at it as just an accident. And accidents happen, right? We'll forgive them and move on. It's just the right thing to do.

Now frustration beaters, as my Granddaddy always said, "Go learn, lead, and lay the way to a better world for all of us." Remember that we shall allow no man nor any woman to belittle our souls by making us hate them. Nope. It just isn't going to happen! We're too good for that, and we know it! And once again, thanks in advance for all that you do, and all that you will do…

CHAPTER EIGHTEEN
OUR CREATOR DOESN'T CREATE JUNK!

L ately, I've been reminded of how easy it is sometimes to feel a little worn down or used up. Sadly, sometimes these feelings can happen when we haven't even had a chance to get up and going. Sometimes it's just hard to feel good about ourselves because this world so rarely goes the way we want it to. But, if we are wise, I believe we'll come to understand that our Creator doesn't create junk. And if our Creator doesn't create garbage, then we all must have some real value, regardless of how we feel about ourselves, or what is going on in our lives at the moment.

So even though our lives don't usually go the way we want them to, believe it or not, they are probably going the way we need them to keep learning and growing. We have to keep telling ourselves that there must be some lessons that we need to learn still. That's all it is… just some more lessons that we need to learn.

Now the problem with still needing to learn some lessons is that it puts these unlearned lessons smack dab right in the middle of our face, which painfully reminds us that there are still some things that we don't know. And for many of us, when we're standing face-to-face with those things that we don't know, we can't help but feel bad about ourselves because… well… we don't know those things.

Let's not be so hard on ourselves and let's come to understand that thoughts come before emotions. And if thoughts come before emotions, and we can change our thoughts, then these different thoughts in return will change our emotions, which will change the way we feel. We don't have to feel bad just because we don't know something. We can think something different and then feel something different about the things we don't know yet.

I would like all of us to change our paradigm, or model, on how we view not knowing something yet. Let's stop telling ourselves that we're stupid or must be junk because we don't know some things. Let's change the story we tell ourselves. Let's start a new story that begins with our Creator doesn't create junk. Continue that story with life's stumbling blocks are temporary. They are just merely a few things that we don't know yet… 'Yet' is the key word here because, given some time and guidance, we will know and understand these lessons. I guarantee it.

You see, this shift from feeling stupid and worthless to feeling capable and valuable is both great and powerful for all of us. We all have the vast capabilities of learning what we don't know yet. We can make this significant shift in our thinking and in the way we talk to ourselves. Let's no longer tell ourselves that others are better than us. Let's also stop telling ourselves that somehow we must have gotten the short end of the stick in life.

Our new paradigm, consisting of our new positive self-talk, will remind us that our Creator doesn't create junk. And since he created us, we can't possibly be junk. We must be nothing but good. All of us have value and are capable of some pretty amazing things. The challenge here is that we don't know what we're capable of yet. Ah… there goes that 'yet' word again. Yet means that there is still hope because the game isn't over. Let's stick around and see how this one ends.

I think we'll see that our lot in life will improve right alongside our new and improved self-confidence and abilities once we start believing in ourselves, and with that confidence then take a few more calculated risks. One feeds the other, and we'll find ourselves right in the middle of a never-ending upward flight pattern where our self-confidence will continue to improve and soar. In return, this improved self-confidence will then cause our abilities to grow again. And our improving capabilities will again feed right back into improving our confidence. It's a never-ending cycle of positivity and productivity that spirals us up to the next level in our lives.

Now frustration beaters, as my Granddaddy always said, "Go learn, lead, and lay the way to a better world for all of us." Remember that our Creator doesn't create junk, so we all must be highly-prized people. And once again, thanks in advance for all that you do, and all that you will do…

CHAPTER NINETEEN
OUR PAST DOES NOT EQUAL
OUR FUTURE!

Some people tend to remember the past as the good old days. And others remember the past as anything but good. In considering our future progress, neither way of remembering the past is ideal because our past doesn't equal our future.

Although I do agree that our past should not be forgotten, I also believe that it is in our best interest to remember our personal history and appreciated it for what it is… our past. Basically, if we're trying to build ourselves our best possible life, then our past should not, and must not, dictate our future. It could be a platform to build off of if it's a good one… but once again… it can't dictate our future.

If we are the type of person who is continuously thinking about our past and always living in a state of nostalgia where we constantly are reminded of how good the old days were, then it probably means that at the present we're living in the past instead of in the moment. It also probably means that we're resting a little too much on our laurels or past achievements.

You know, my Granddaddy once told me, "The good old days weren't always so good, and tomorrow ain't as bad as it seems." We should appreciate yesterday, but we should also let go of it so we can reach for the gold with both of our hands that tomorrow has to offer. If we don't have both hands free while trying to reach for tomorrow's opportunities, we may end up letting great opportunities slip through our grasp.

Now if you're the type of person that seems only to remember the failures of yesteryear and does not believe in the good old days, then you too are going to miss some of the golden opportunities of tomorrow. Listen, just because you couldn't do something yesterday, it doesn't mean that you won't be able to do it today, or maybe tomorrow.

I think you'll agree that there was a time when we were all babies, and we couldn't walk upright yet on our own two feet. The small fact that we couldn't even stand upright without falling forward didn't stop us from eventually standing tall and running forward, at full-speed ahead as we got bigger, older, and more capable.

Now I know that some of us have complaints of growing up on the wrong side of the tracks. It's true; life has been hard for some of us. And yes, sometimes it seems that some of us have never gotten any of the breaks. Sadly, some of us have legitimate gripes about not being raised in a loving, nurturing family that would have guided us in the right direction. And I know that many of us believe that we didn't get the proper education or the right opportunity to be around, or grow-up with the right kind of successful people. It seems like some of us can never catch a break.

To all that hardship and lack of opportunity, I say one simple little thing: Our past does not equal our future.

We can leave all that bad luck behind us and start down a new path of prosperity today. We can even run forward, full-speed ahead down a new, better road right now. And we can even tightly grab with both of our hands all those golden opportunities of tomorrow because we now know that our past does not equal our future, right?

Tomorrow's beautiful sunrise is just waiting to be grasped with both hands, taken in, and deeply appreciated. All of us can have a piece of this sunshine if we're willing just to show up and participate in the miracle of a new day. Hey! I have a great idea. Let's be there and let's fully participate in our own new day!

Now frustration beaters, as my Granddaddy always said, "Go learn, lead, and lay the way to a better world for all of us." Let's remember that our past does not equal our future. So go ahead and create a new incredible future for yourself, and subsequently for your loved ones too. And once again, thanks in advance for all that you do, and all that you will do…

CHAPTER TWENTY
EVEN FAILED EFFORT PRODUCES MUSCLE!

Today, a good friend of mine, who had just recently started an exercise routine, expressed how sore her legs were, and how painful it was for her to now walk. It was the second day after her workout, and she told me that the pain was almost unbearable. As a joke, I asked her if she wanted me to help her walk up the stairs. That's when she replied with a painful laugh that climbing up the stairs wasn't the problem. She could manage that. The real problem was trying to come down the stairs. So, it was not the ascending, but rather the descending that caused the most pain and discomfort for her.

Her comment about coming down the stairs being more painful instantly reminded me of my old workout days and how I always felt it more in my legs when I was coming down from a hike in the mountains than when I had previously been going up the mountain. I started reminiscing about some of my old days in the gym, too. Memories flooded my brain of lifting up a weight in which my muscles were forced to work really hard while it was contracting during the positive or upward part of the exercise. Just in case you wanted to know, the lifting the weight up is called the concentric portion of an exercise. I have to say though, that I vividly remember the lowering of the weight, which was called the eccentric part of the exercise, always left me sorer.

When my workout buddies and I really wanted to shock our muscles into some new growth, for short periods of time we would mainly focus on the controlled, slow, and lowering of the weights after they had just been hoisted up. This advanced technique of weight lifters is called negative reps. The weight is just too heavy or the muscle has become too fatigued to lift the weight up anymore. However, with some help, our muscles are still able to endure the slow, lowering of the weight.

As we saw above, this eccentric concept can also be applied to coming down from the mountain when one is exhausted and unable to climb any higher. The short training durations of negatives or slow descents, which usually ended up with muscle failure in the gym, was guaranteed to blast our muscles. And the soreness over the next few days made sure that we remembered those workouts.

This little story above about muscle failure and failed effort has much wider reaching powers than the typical gym rat, though. You see, it's not just the fitness world that has this phenomenon of slow descents, negative reps, and failed efforts that are producing bigger, and stronger muscles. In life, our failed efforts produce larger courage muscles, too. These bigger and stronger courage muscles produce more human capabilities that continue to grow with each future failed effort into more and more human capacity.

Listen, we all know the world is filled with everyday people who would like to try to avoid failed effort. And for the most part, we can't blame them, huh? However, every once in a while, someone will pass through our lives who catches our attention. We can't help but notice that there is something different about this particular person. Is it their broader shoulders and firmer arms? Or is it just the presence of confidence and determination? Either way, I'm sure what produces standout qualities in these special people is a lot of failed effort, negative reps, and many descents when they would rather have been climbing up.

These special people who have caught our attention have learned to accept, deal with, and even look forward to the pain of negative reps, failed effort, and descents. These special people deal very successfully with the pains of life brought on by adversity and negativity. In bearing the pain, they already know that they are someone who is special, and someone who is going somewhere in life. Their daily winning habits, positive outlook in life, and the ability to deal with the pain of trying to succeed have built up their life-muscles.

These winners know that for them to be truly happy, they need to fulfill their true potential by taking their life to the next level through the advanced technique of openly accepting things that often causes pain and rejection. Successful people deal with the pain until it no longer feels like the enemy, but rather as an old acquaintance. They don't see the suffering of failed attempts, failed efforts, and descents as something to be avoided anymore. But, instead, they know the pain and adversity is something to embrace and look forward to now because it brings along with it the amazing progress, self-satisfaction, leadership skills, and quality of life that so few others will ever get the chance to truly experience and enjoy.

Now frustration beaters, as my Granddaddy always said, "Go learn, lead, and lay the way to a better world for all of us. Remember that even failed effort produces muscle. So stop being so negative about it. And once again, thanks in advance for all that you do, and all that you will do…

CHAPTER TWENTY-ONE
FEAR IS A HORRIBLE USE OF OUR
IMAGINATION!

D o you remember when people used to ask what you wanted to be when you grew up? Many of the typical answers that we imagined consisted of courageous jobs like a fireman, astronaut, movie star, or even sports star, right?

All the cool careers and lifestyles that we came up with required great imagination from us when we were just mere children. All of these career dreams consisted of future lives of skill and courage where the concept of fear did not run our lives, nor even quickly run through our minds.

Please think about this for a moment. When we were children, and someone asked us what we wanted to be when we grew up, did fear overtake our bodies and minds? Probably not! Most likely not! Definitely not! Courage and future possibilities overtook our bodies and minds instead, as we easily stood a little taller. And then fearlessly spouted off what we wanted to be when we grew up.

So what happened to our empowering imagination, as we grew older? Where along the line did fear creep into our existence and take up permanent residency in our minds and bodies? Somehow and somewhere, a lot of doubt crept into our being and is now part of our everyday lives. Whether we know it or not, we have learned to partner up with fear. Sadly, this partner is a bad dude, and he is pushing out the wonderful imagination of good and wonder that we used to have.

The unfortunate thing though, is that fear is mostly a learned response to our environment. Well, I guess this could be a good thing in some ways because if we can learn fear, then we can also unlearn fear.

As babies, we aren't born with all of the fears that we now have as adults. As babies, our only innate fears were loud noises and falling. All other concerns that we have today were learned over time. So outside of these two fears of loud noises and falling, which shouldn't really have any kind of a hold on us now as big people, we should be basically fear free adults, right? Hmm…

The beautiful thing is that when we're young before we learn all this fear, we're basically optimizing our imagination by dreaming about all the possibilities that life has to offer us--- like being a fireman, astronaut, movie star, or sports star. Unfortunately, somewhere along the way all these dreams fade away and are replaced by the limitations of fears and failures, particularly painful past failures.

Somehow life got our imagination to jump the rail of possibilities and land on a fear-ridden line of impossibilities, pain, and a quiet life of desperation. Now we're always looking around the next corner for the boogeyman or anything else that may hurt us, or embarrass us.

Let's stop and think about this for a minute. Are we spending so much time worrying about what could go wrong that we have forgotten how to dream about what could go right? What could we be if we believed that anything was possible again?

Can you remember what you wanted to be when you were little? Maybe not. Maybe you've been using your imagination over the years for the less-fulfilling things in life… Now it's time to get back on track and get back our childhood dreams again! Come on… try hard to remember what you wanted to be as a child…come on… think…. What did the young you want to be when you only saw life through the glasses of possibilities and superheroes?

Do you remember now? Good! Well, what's stopping you from having that dream again? Come on, you're not five years old anymore. You're now older and actually better equipped to reach for your dreams than you were back when you gave up on your dreams…

Your renewed positive and limitless imagination of being something great where fear isn't even considered is still inside of you. You're bigger, older, stronger, faster, smarter, and everything else that adds up to being more capable now than when you were younger and let the dream get away.

We can do this. We just have to stop using our imagination in a counterproductive way. We have to start using it again in a way that it serves us like it used to; like the way our Creator meant it to be used. Let's begin right now to use our imagination in a way that is full of possibilities! Let's start using it in a way that will make this world a better place for all of us and everyone else that we come into contact with! Come on… let's wake up that imagination and let's get our dreams back on track!

Now frustration beaters, as my Granddaddy always said, "Go learn, lead, and lay the way to a better world for all of us." Remember that fear is a horrible waste of our imagination. And once again, thanks in advance for all that you do, and all that you will do…

BONUS CHAPTERS

BONUS CHAPTER ONE
WE CAN CHOOSE TO GET BITTER
OR BETTER!

Have you ever bitten into a lemon? Wow! Did your taste buds on both the left and right side of the back of your tongue just fire off? Did this memory of a sour lemon cause you to salivate and form extra fluid in the back sides of your mouth? Did you just notice yourself wincing a little bit, too? I did.

Now, if you have never experienced firsthand biting into a lemon, guess what? I have some powerful news for you, too! The bitterness of a sour experience doesn't just stop with you or any other person who may be biting into a lemon.

For example, have you ever seen someone else bite into a lemon? If not, then go ahead and just take a moment to imagine one of your friends or family members getting ready to bite into a big, yellow, juicy lemon. Can you see them cutting the lemon into small, bite-size pieces? Now, can you see him or her putting one of the lemon wedges into their mouth? Can you see them wincing now? Oooohhhh…. What just happened? Did your salivary glands on the right and left backside of your tongue just fire off too? Did you feel yourself also wincing at that imaginary bitter experience your friend or family member was experiencing when he or she bit into that sour lemon? I bet you did if you truly imagined it in detail.

Okay, now stop wincing and start paying attention to what you are about to digest next. It's just a cold hard fact folks that life is going to serve every one of us lemons from time to time. As this simulated experience just showed us, it is really easy for these lemons to sour our lives, leave a bad taste in our mouths, and create a lot of bitterness within ourselves.

Furthermore, not only can life's lemons cause us discomfort when some of life's unpleasant things are forced upon us, but these lemons can also cause us to wear a sour puss and be bitter even when someone other than us is dished up a serving. It's very easy to become sour on life and to get bitter toward a lot of things. It's also very painful when we give in and allow ourselves to become victims of life's lemons. Don't be a victim, be a victor for yourself and for others!

Let's not get bitter! Let's get better! We do, in fact, have a choice. Listen, I know we're all still part of the animal kingdom, but fortunately for us, evolution has given us the amazing gift of being able to pause and think about what we want to do with life's lemons. As evolved human beings, we are no longer caged into mindlessly responding to life's lemony stimuli as though we were Pavlov's dog.

We humans can examine a problem, and if our present self isn't up to the task of solving it, we can better our self by asking others for advice, and maybe even help. In addition, we could also go to the Internet and search for information on how to overcome this particular problem. Once we have found the information necessary to deal with our problem, we then can successfully act or behave in a way that will move us through and beyond the particular problem that we are facing.

Once we are successful beyond this problem, I think we will no longer be bitter about this old problem. As a matter of fact, now we should be better because we conquered the challenge. Don't get bitter! Get better! When life serves us lemons, let's figure out a way to make lemonade, and then actually really make that lemonade.

Ahh... the delightful refreshing and reinvigorating reward of becoming better! Can you taste that sweet success, yet?

Now frustration beaters, as my Granddaddy always said, "Go learn, lead, and lay the way to a better world for all of us." Remember that when life serves us lemons, we can choose to get bitter or get better. Let's choose better! And once again, thanks in advance for all that you do, and all that you will do...

BONUS CHAPTER TWO
WE DON'T HAVE TO BE A VICTIM OF
OUR CIRCUMSTANCES!

O kay. I admit it. This world isn't always easy for us. Sometimes it seems like the deck of cards is stacked against us. Too frequently we're unwillingly a victim of some smooth talking slickster or some crazy circumstances that we just don't have any control over. "Life isn't fair" we tend to tell ourselves when faced with these injustices.

"True. Very true," I say. You're right. Life isn't fair, and life has never been fair. Just think about it… What happens when a fly flies innocently by a frog? Yup! It gets eaten. Life certainly wasn't fair for that poor fly, was it? I mean, let's really think about this. What did that innocent little fly do to that big old mean frog in the first place? Right! Nothing! It was unfair to that fly, wasn't it? Boy, I bet right now, we're all glad that we're not flies.

Well, we certainly aren't flies. And we usually don't have to worry much about being eaten alive by another creature. Life for us humans is indeed unfair sometimes, but it's rarely ever as unfair it was for that poor fly. Hey, to tell you the truth, we're rarely victimized to the degree that that poor fly was because we're humans, and we have a lot of advantages over the rest of the animal kingdom.

Come to think of it, the fact that we humans are on the top of the food chain and have all sorts of advantages over the rest of the animal kingdom, probably isn't fair to them, right? Our circumstances are different than the rest of the animals, but that's just how the world spins. In the wild, that fly couldn't help being a victim of its circumstances in which it found itself in when it flew by a frog. We humans don't live in the wild. And we don't have to be victims of our circumstances, in the same way, the rest of the animal kingdom does because our living arrangements are rarely as dire and disadvantaged as theirs.

It's not often that our circumstances force us to face life and death situations like the rest of the animal kingdom does on a daily basis. And when our conditions do tend to be on the bad side, we almost always have choices that we can make to better our situation. The fly flying by the frog doesn't have the ability like us humans to make life-improving decisions once that frog snaps its tongue out of its mouth. Can you imagine what us humans would do if a little frog snapped its tongue out of its mouth towards us? We'd probably say, "Ah… look how cute he is!" We'd probably even mimic the cute little frog by saying, "Ribbit. Ribbit".

Life's not fair, huh? It sure isn't! Heck, if we really think about it, even if a man-eating lion made a start toward us, chances are that that lion would be stopped at the zoo's fence that keeps him in its place. And even if we were in the wild, chances are that there would be someone standing beside us with a weapon to protect us. Life just isn't fair for all those animals that find themselves underneath us on the food chain. And yet, I've never heard any of those other animals complain about life as humans do. We humans, who sit at the top of the food chain, might be the only animals who do complain about how unfair life is.

In considering this comparison with some of the other animals in the animal kingdom, do we really still think we humans are helpless victims of our circumstances? Not by a long shot, buddy! As I mentioned above, our circumstances usually aren't as dire as the other animals that roam this planet, if they're even allowed to truly roam... Furthermore, we typically have some choices, options, and help available to us to will improve our circumstances, right? Do the other animals in the animal kingdom get that? I don't think so...

Now frustration beaters, as my Granddaddy always said, "Go learn, lead, and lay the way to a better world for all of us." Remember that we indeed are the lucky ones because we don't have to be victimized by our circumstances. And once again, thanks for all that you do, and all that you will do...

9 7 9 8 7 4 5 2 5 5 8 3 0